1. In Garments All Red

IN GARMENTS ALL RED

IN GARMENTS ALL RED

The Life Story of St. Maria Goretti

by Godfrey Poage, C.P.

St. Paul
Editions

Nihil Obstat
    Kilian Dooley, C.P., Ph.D.
    Censor Deputatus

Imprimi Potest
    James Patrick White, C.P.
    Provincial of Holy Cross Province

Imprimatur
    ✚ Samuel Cardinal Stritch, D.D.
    Archbishop of Chicago

Poage, Godfrey Robert, 1920-
    In garments all red.

    1. Maria Goretti, Saint, 1890-1902. 2. Christian saints—Italy—Biography. I. Title.
    BX4700.M368P6   1977   282'.092'4   [B]   77-4485

Copyright © 1977, by the Daughters of St. Paul

Printed in the U.S.A. by the Daughters of St. Paul
50 St. Paul's Ave., Boston, Ma. 02130

The Daughters of St. Paul are an international religious congregation serving the Church with the communications media.

The moment Maria died witnesses claimed that the Church bells in Nettuno could be heard announcing Vespers. The signal to ring those bells was the priest intoning the Antiphon for the Feast of the Precious Blood, which happened to be: "Who is this that comes into heaven... this beautiful one in garments all red, with clothing stained like one who has tread the winepress?"

The words are from the 63rd Chapter of Isaiah and refer to Christ, but they are also so aptly attributed to Maria Goretti, whence the title of her biography
IN GARMENTS ALL RED

Dedication
To Mary,
Queen of Martyrs

Contents

	Allocution of Pope Pius XII on Maria Goretti	9
	Picture Section	17
	Prologue	33
1.	Journey For Maria	45
2.	Home in The Swampland	51
3.	Coming of The Serenellis	57
4.	Misunderstanding and Warning	63
5.	Maria's Happiest Day	69
6.	The Little Woman	75
7.	The Angel of Darkness	79
8.	Even To Blood	85
9.	Hours of Pain	93
10.	The Final Struggle	99
	Epilogue	107
	Model of Youth	109
	Heaven on the Swampland	115

Characters

Goretti Family:

Luigi	Father
Assunta	Mother
Tonino	Son
Angelo	Son
Maria	Daughter
Mariano	Son
Allessandro	Son
Ersilia	Daughter
Theresa	Daughter

Cimarelli Family:

Theresa	Sister
Dominico	Brother

Serenelli Family:

Giovanni	Father
Alexander	Son

Allocution of Pope Pius XII

The life story of Maria Goretti resembles very closely that of St. Agnes. The features of the Roman martyr and those of this little girl of Corinaldo shine with the same charm. The souls of both emit the same fragrance. Yet there is danger in that a too superficial, too natural conception of their adolescent beauty and candor overshadow their characteristic virtue which is *strength of soul*. Their youth set off in a more living, more radiant light, the courage of the martyr and the courage of the virgin. Courage was both the result and safeguard of their virginity.

Those individuals err greatly who consider virginity as the effect of ignorance or the simplicity of small souls. They who smile with pity on virgins, thinking of them as passionless, ardorless, or inexperienced, misjudge their true worth. How can he or she, who has ceded without struggle, imagine the courage required to dominate through long years, without an instant of weakness, the secret excitations and troubles of sense and heart. Since original sin, human nature is in a ferment, troubled by a thousand curiosities to see, to hear, to taste and feel. Great courage is required to resist those curiosities which present to the lips the intoxicating cup and exude the deadly scent of the flowers of evil. Great courage is required to live firmly, superior to every temptation, superior to every threat, superior to all seductive and taunting influences amidst the baseness of the world.

Agnes in the whirl of pagan society, and Maria Goretti in the proximity of passionate, shameless men, were neither ignorant nor insensible. They had strong hearts, strong in that supernatural strength whose germ every Christian received in holy Baptism. Thanks to a diligent and sustained education, in affectionable collaboration of parents and children, that germ grew into manifold fruit of virtue and blessing.

In the humble family circle where Maria Goretti grew up, her education was simple but careful, and she corresponded to it perfectly. The testimony of her mother that this little girl never caused her the least voluntary displeasure is proof enough. And who can read without emotion the declaration of her murderer that he never ascertained in Maria Goretti a failing in the law of God!

Our Saint was a valiant girl. She knew, she understood, and that is why she preferred to die. Her twelfth year was not completed when she fell martyred. Yet, what discernment, what prudence, what energy she displayed! Though but a girl, conscious of danger, she watched night and day in defense of her honor, and in persevering prayer recommended the lily of her purity to the Virgin of virgins. No! Hers was not a small, weak soul. She is a heroine who in the clutch of a murderer and under the knife of an assassin thought not of her suffering but resolutely repelled sin with horror.

Thank God, there are still many more like her. They are more numerous than is thought or mentioned, because they make no display of their seriousness and virtue as other girls do of their levity and disorders. Raised by Christian parents they modestly pass happy and joyful down the streets of our cities and in the byways of our countrysides. They pursue domestic, professional, scholarly and charitable duties. They know how to make their pleasing manner loved, and their unbending dignity respected.

Beyond all doubt there are still very many of these girls. They would be still more numerous, if there were more devoted interest, and true kindness in parents, and more confident docility in children.

How many concessions are made, how many capitulations are undergone! Passing whims they are, and heedlessness quickly obliterates them at first. But their humiliating remembrance reappears later with torturing remorse like gas bubbles coming to the surface of a stagnant pond. Their bitterness even after pardon is never completely assuaged. Worse still are those misfortunes that cast so many girls into the bottom of the abyss, tragedies that terminate in hopeless death, progressive falls that end in a final fall, humanly irreparable.

In view of such lamentable weaknesses, so many miserable falls, we must admire the strength of pure hearts. It is a mysterious power. It is a strength that outstrips the limits of human nature, and often enough the limits of ordinary christian virtue. It is the bond of love for the Divine Spouse. It is the strength of the soul which spurns whoever dares test its fidelity or threatens the purity of its affections.

Maria Goretti showed herself to be such a one no less in her life than in her martyrdom. Shall we then class her with Agnes and Cecilia, Catherine of Siena and Therese of the Child Jesus, and many others who, with heroic abnegation and the blessings of their virginity, wore the nuptial ring that bound them to their heavenly Spouse? But Maria Goretti was only a child and there is no reason for asserting that she would have consecrated herself to the Lord by the Vow of Virginity. There is nothing to indicate that, as she advanced in years, she would not have followed the path of so many other young women who bring the flower of their integrity to the altar in order to give God new adorers through holy Matrimony—chosen members to the human family, devoted children to the Church, future saints to heaven. Yet Christ knew well that He had chosen her for His Own. Without thought of the future she had given herself entirely to Him in her heart. She desired but one thing: fidelity to Christ at any price, even at the cost of her life. Never for anything in the world, would she violate the Divine Law.

She was not merely an ingenuous, candid girl, instinctively frightened at the menace of sin as at the sight of a snake (Eccl. 21/2). She may not be compared to the legendary ermine that permitted itself to be killed rather than soil its paw on the muddy road. She was not guided simply by natural sentiment of reserve. Though still very young we can catch a glimpse in her of a deep, intense love for Our Divine Redeemer. She had not yet learned to read. Poverty and a distance kept her from school. But her love knew neither difficulty nor distance. She set about her household tasks more courageously and hurried off to attend Catechism lessons far away. In order to receive her Eucharistic Jesus, she did not hesitate to travel a long dusty road in midsummer under a scorching sun. "I don't know at what time tomorrow I will receive Holy Communion," she said one day. That tomorrow was to come and that Holy Communion. But what a tomorrow! and what a Communion! The very afternoon of that day on which she spoke those words, she shed her blood in order to remain faithful to the Spouse of virgins.

It is not yet a half-century since the pathetic death of Maria Goretti. The period has been one seething with stormy vicissitudes and sudden revolts. Radical transformations have upset the life of our young girls and women. We have fully pointed out on other occasions how within the past fifty years, woman has departed from the retirement and reserve that formerly characterized her life, and has launched out into the domain of public life, including military service. That transformation has taken place with pitiless speed.

Lest such deep and speedy alternation effect most grave consequences to the religion and morals of woman, it is necessary at the same time and in equal degree to strengthen in her those deep personal and supernatural values that shone in our Saint. There must be a spirit of faith and modesty —not mere natural modesty and decency—but a carefully cultivated Christian virtue. Those who have at heart the welfare of human society, as well as the temporal and eternal salvation of woman, must resolutely demand that public morality protect the honor and dignity of woman. What is the present situation? Are you wrong in affirming that in this regard perhaps no epoch has failed as ours in its duty toward woman?

Thus the cry of our Savior rises to our lips: "Woe to the world because of scandals!" (Matt. 18/7). Woe to those guilty perverters—authors of corrupt novels, newspapers, periodicals, theatres, films, indecent styles! Woe to those young men who, with artful and thoughtless cruelty, introduce deadly infection into a virgin heart! Woe to those fathers and mothers lacking in energy and prudence, who cede to the caprices of their children and surrender that paternal authority written on the brow of man and wife as a reelection of the divine Majesty. Woe also to that multitude of Christians in name only, who could take a stand and would see legions of upright and virtuous followers mass behind them ready to battle scandal by every means! Legal justice punishes the slayer of a child, and it has duty to do so. But what human legislation could or would dare, if it chose to do so, punish those who furnished the weapon to the slayer's hand, those who encouraged him therein, or were indifferent, or even with indulgent smile left him be? And yet they are really the more guilty. The terrible justice of God weighs heavily on them, those wilful perverters or indolent accomplices!

Has human power, then, no strength to move and convert those corrupt and corrupting hearts? Has it no strength to open the eyes and arouse those many careless, timid Christians from their torpor? We hope this martyr's blood, and the tears of her repentant and penitent murderer will perform that miracle!

Our hope is not in vain. Thus we do not hesitate to repeat here the words of the Apostle Paul: "Where sin hath abounded, grace hath more abounded" (Rom. 15/20). Behold the Church! Now the ranks of those who believe, who pray, who impose heavy sacrifices on themselves grow and form even among the youth! They squarely reject what God wills not to be. They are restless until they have brought back to Christ and His law their friends and associates who have become estranged from God. They are Our comfort and Our Joy.

Full of such confidence let us raise up our eyes to heaven and consider the resplendent host of those who have washed their robes in the Blood of the Lamb, that host led by the Virgin of virgins. Let us call upon their intercession. Let us unite our humble prayers to theirs in order to bring down upon the earth the abundant shower of grace that cleanses and strengthens.

As a pledge of that grace We accord you with all Our heart Our Apostolic Blessing.

Pope Pius XII

The Reliquary of St. Maria Goretti now preserved at the Church of Our Lady of Grace, Nettuno, Italy.

Parish Church at Nettuno where Maria
made her first Communion.

Goretti home in Ferriere di Conca, near Anzio,
where martyrdom took place.

"When will Jesus come again"—first thought of Maria Goretti on the day of her first Communion.

All Ferriere had part in her adornment on that great day.

Though little more than a child, Maria was burdened with care of the home.

No fields seemed more barren when the Gorettis began planting.

On trips to Nettuno Maria refound her childhood gaiety.

Maria and Alexander watch the surf at Anzio,
a short distance from home.

"Maria come here!"...Too well does she understand his meaning.

After the attack Alexander is led away to prison chained between two mounted police.

At the hospital the doctors discovered
fourteen wounds in breast and abdomen.

Maria's mother and family view Reliquary
when exposed the first time for public
veneration.

After being released, Alexander, Maria's attacker, worked as a handyman at the Capuchin Monastery at Ascoli.

Sanctuary of Our Lady of Graces in Nettuno where Maria's remains were placed in a new coffin.

Family views beatification ceremonies: left to right, her sisters Theresa, Ersilia, mother, nephew, brother Mariano

Maria crowned with glory at beatification ceremonies in St. Peter's, 1947

Passionist Fathers, custodians of Reliquary, touch religious articles to body.

Holy Father publicly prays to new beata, Maria Goretti.

Forty-eight years after her death, Maria Goretti is canonized in first outdoor ceremony of its kind. Holy Father at Papal Throne in background.

Part of the crowd of over two hundred thousand Holy Year pilgrims who thronged piazza of St. Peter's to witness ceremony on June 24, 1950.

Assunta, first mother ever to witness canonization of daughter, follows ceremony from window in Vatican.

The Holy Father proclaiming Maria a Saint.

Painting of Maria Goretti in glory, borne triumphantly through crowd at canonization.

Family and Promoters of Cause assist at Mass in honor of St. Maria Goretti from special box near Main Altar.

Maria receives highest honors Church can bestow.

Prologue

They say that if you go from Rome to Nettuno by way of Campo Morto and Ferriere, you will hear everybody along the way speaking of Maria Goretti. Through that countryside she has become legendary. The old people remember her; the young have learned to love her.

One old lady tells us proudly that she made her First Communion with Maria. Another met the saint many times on market day. A farmer claims she came to him, a few days before her death, to return a sickle that Alexander Serenelli had borrowed. A seamstress remembers Maria coming to her mother's shop to try on a dress the very morning of the day Alexander attacked her. Not yet a half century after her death Maria Goretti lives in the hearts of her people.

When I asked her neighbor, Theresa Cimarelli, about her, she exclaimed: "Madonna mia! I used to see her every day as she passed by the door to get water from the well. But she never stopped. She was a serious girl. She went and came quickly and busily, and there was no reproach when we nicknamed her *the little old Lady*."

"Maria was always modest and reserved. We all liked her and deep down we admired her. She was more religious than the rest of us. I was just a girl then and would that I had followed her example! But at that age most of us are senseless. We scarcely know what we are doing. We seek pleasure and popularity. We permit ourselves to be distracted from better things."

She hesitated a moment and sighed. She seemed to have more to say but refrained.

"Come in," she invited, "and meet Domenico." I needed no urging, for Theresa Cimarelli and her brother-in-law had lived through the events of our story and were witnesses of many of its details.

I sat down at the simple wooden table and looked about the plainly furnished room. Theresa went to the back door and called: "Domenico . . . Domenico!"

There was no reply, but the wood chopping in a nearby shed ceased. The old lady then drew out a jug of wine and set glasses on the table. In a moment Domenico entered.

Domenico was up in years and walked with a stoop. The sun had tanned his skin. His blue work-clothes gave off the pungent ordor of sheep. He offered me his hand in honest welcome, drew up a chair, and filled the glasses with the cool sparkling wine. Theresa then explained to him my interest in the life of Maria Goretti and urged him to help her retell the story.

The pleasure of these two friends of Maria having a foreigner in their home and being able to retell the drama they had witnessed was all too evident. They seemed to relive those tragic scenes. No detail was omitted.

Theresa and Domenico have not left Ferriere since Maria's death, and I can only guess the hundreds of times they have gone over the terrible story together in the past forty-five years. All I did was listen. They told the tale from beginning to end and concluded with these words:

"The day of the burial of Maria—and it was a real triumph—the whole populace of Nettuno accompanied the body to the cemetery. Her mother, Assunta, came back to Ferriere. She did not stay long. You understand. She could no longer live in the house that recalled such sad memories. So she left this region and returned to Corinaldo with her children. Old Serenelli disappeared too. No one ever heard of him again. The Ferriere farm was once more abandoned and once more known as "the old cheese factory".

"What about Alexander?" I asked. I was eager to know how he had paid for his crime.

"Alexander!" said Domenico. "That is a whole story in itself! First of all, he was imprisoned at Nettuno. They then transferred him to the Regina-Coeli at Rome, where his trial began. I was called in as witness. Alexander was arrogant and cynical before his judges. He denied up and down that he had anything to do with the crime. He pretended that he was the object of grave injustice and was highly indignant that anyone should accuse him of such a transgression. But the evidence was overwhelming. Though he put on a brave front he was not able to escape, and finally made an avowal of guilt. Then to influence the judges he tried to hide behind the curtain of insanity, calling in the cases of his mother and brother. Doctors examined him and declared he was responsible for his own actions. But since he was a minor, he was sentenced to only thirty years of hard labor.

"I heard that he was sent first to the penitentiary of Noto in Sicily. It was said that in the beginning of his term he seemed happy as a bird in its cage. He even composed a song with the refrain:

"Take courage, Serenelli,

Banish your fears,

You'll be welcomed home with cheers.'

"His conscience did not seem to be troubled with remorse, until one day a priest came to see him. As the guards brought Alexander in for the talk, fierce anger seized hold of him and he yelled wildly: 'It was all your fault I lost her! You and your teachings!'

"The priest tried to reason with him, appealing to God's infinite mercy and Maria's own generous pardon. But Alexander only howled like a maniac and lunged at the priest. As the guards pulled him away, the priest said: 'Soon, Alexander, you will want me. Maria will see to that'.

" 'Never', the prisoner screamed. 'I'll never want you, never!'

"In the days that followed Alexander could not sleep. He grew nervous and lost his appetite. Then one night in the solitude of his cell Maria appeared to him. Terrified, he screamed for the guards. When they arrived, he was almost incoherent.

" 'I saw her! I saw her!', he gasped in great excitement. 'I saw Maria dressed in dazzling white gathering beautiful lilies in a garden and handing them to me. As I took them from her outstretched hands, they were transformed into small lights that glowed like candles. Call the priest! Bring me the priest!'

"It was now the jailers turn to laugh. Write to the priest if you have something to say, they answered callously. So Alexander knelt on the floor of his cell and scrawled the following note:

'I am deeply sorry for what has happened.
I have taken the life of an innocent girl
whose one aim was to save her purity,
shedding her blood rather than give in to
my sinful desires. I publicly retract
the evil I have done and beg pardon of
God and of the stricken family. One hope
encourages me—that I also may one day

obtain God's pardon as so many others have.'

Alexander Serenelli
November 10, 1910

"This note from Alexander only confirmed our belief that Maria was a saint, a real martyr. The word of how she had died passed throughout the country and people started making pilgrimages to her tomb. We prayed to her and asked for cures . . . and miracles were performed."

I looked skeptical. Domenico noted my astonishment and continued.

"I saw a boy of Nettuno brought to the cemetery by his mother. He was eaten away by consumption, a wasted child, Hermano by name. They prayed at Maria's grave and the boy left the cemetery cured. From that day forward he grew strong and healthy and when he was twenty he was drafted for military service.

"I heard also of a man in Rome who was instantly cured of an internal abscess by calling on Maria. His doctor attested to the fact. I could tell you of many other incidents as equally marvelous; for instance, the Lady Miscetti, who was to undergo an operation, was cured of a cyst in her thyroid gland after praying to Maria. Then, too, a Sicilian priest was freed of a serious kidney condition by the same prayer. But what does it matter after all? Miracles don't change anything. When one has chosen to die rather than to offend God, one is a martyr and that's that! That's why our little Maria is a saint today".

I was going from one surprise to another. The good Domenico seemed to know his history. He was full of his theme. He was not just talking. He was expatiating with remarkable ease. I began to perceive that he had been more closely involved in the affair, though I did not know where he was leading: "Did you say she has been canonized?", I asked innocently.

He was more astonished than I. "You mean you think she doesn't deserve it?", he asked.

"No," I replied, "but why has it taken so long?"

"Rome," he answered, "moves slowly in canonizing saints. There are inquiries, depositions, discussions . . . and then all the data is put away in the archives. Then some fine day, the case is taken up again. New inquests, new depositions, new discussions are brought forth. This time it seems we have something. It is going to succeed. And then . . . disappointment! The devil's advocate finds an objection: Maria should have disclosed her secret . . . she hesitated before pardoning her assassin . . . she may have provoked him. Such false reasons hold up the process. Thus we have to be patient for years. But the Church knows best.

"I was called in several times," Domenico continued, "to testify. Police, doctors, nurses were also called in—everyone, in fact, who had something to say. Assunta, naturally, was the first defendant of her daughter. We were all of one mind. Maria was innocent; she had given proof of her heroic courage. But that was not enough. One witness was wanting—the only one able to settle the question, her murderer, Alexander!

"After thirty-five years he came back to Corinaldo, a changed man. Maria's prayers had won him completely. His prison sentence had been served and he wanted to repair the evil of his crime. He who formerly had taken every means to exonerate himself, now humbly admitted his guilt. It is no small thing when a criminal rises to the defense of his victim. He affirmed that she had been altogether innocent. She had opposed his brutal passion with all her strength. Finally, he obtained what he sought—her vindication.

"He even went further than that and on Christmas eve of 1937 begged pardon of Assunta. The old mother's voice broke as she fought back the tears: Maria forgave you, Alexander, she answered, so how could I possibly refuse?

"The following morning, Christmas day, the parish Church at Corinaldo was filled to overflowing as Assunta and Alexander entered side by side. A hush fell on everyone. At the communion rail, Alexander turned and all eyes were upon him.

" 'I have sinned deeply', he said. 'I have murdered an innocent girl who loved virtue more than life. May God forgive me! I beg your pardon!'

"After this I heard that Alexander retired to a Capuchin Monastery of Ascoli, where he put on the habit of a tertiary. He's working there now as gardener, tending the flowers. Lilies are his favorites . . ."

Domenico seemed to have finished his tale. I had listened with intense interest. What a story! And yet all so true.

I knew from a friend of mine who had been present, what popular enthusiasm accompanied the Canonization on June 24, 1950. In front of that great throng an old lady, Assunta, had the place of honor. She raised her head, with tear-filled eyes, saw the veil removed from the picture of Maria just as His Holiness Pope Pius XII proclaimed her to be a saint.

The excited Holy Year throng behind expressed her thoughts. "There she is . . . Maria Goretti . . . Saint Maria Goretti!" Thus the drama of Ferriere has terminated in the glory of the Vatican!

"For me," mused Domenico, she will always be our little Maria. I wouldn't know how to call her otherwise. You understand, we were her neighbors. We lived in the house next to hers. I was twenty years old when she died."

Domenico fell to silent musing. He was tired reminiscing. The village clock struck eleven. I was about to leave when the door opened. A little girl looked in. At the sight of me she hesitated, doubtful as to whether she should enter or withdraw. A great straw hat haloed her head. She wore a blue and white summer dress, which scarcely reached her knees. Her bare arms were tanned with the sun.

"Angelina, come in and speak to Father," said Domenico. "Don't stand there gaping."

"This is my granddaughter," he explained.

The little girl seemed timid, frightened at my presence. But she came over and shook hands with smiling grace. Then she went out by the back door.

I rose and thanked Domenico and Theresa for their kindness and hospitality. But for them my story would have been incomplete. I paused a moment on the threshold to adjust my eyes to the burning sunlight, and then set off resolutely for the long, hot walk to Nettuno. Maria had made the journey before me and it seemed I was following her. No one else was on the road at that time of day, and I walked alone with my thoughts.

Maria ... Angelina—girl of yesterday ... youngster of today.

Styles have changed. The light dress and straw hat have replaced the heavy skirts and shawls. Long braided hair has given place to a simple cut and combing. Adornments and mannerisms have altered. But deep down there has been no transformation. A girl's real beauty is still within. It is a thing of her soul, shining through her pure eyes and radiating her whole body. It is something with which she makes men aware of the truth and beauty and goodness of God by reflecting that beauty and goodness in herself.

At Nettuno in the Basilica of Our Lady of Grace, I visited the shrine where the body of Maria Goretti is preserved. A young man was there, kneeling in prayer. He thought he was alone, and I saw him lean over reverently to kiss the marble in front of her reliquary. Then he blessed himself and left, buoyed up with the confidence that Maria, the new patroness of Catholic youth, would help him gain a victory over himself.

This is more than enough for the triumphs of today! Let us go back some fifty years to the more important story of how Maria actually won her victory over sin . . .

1.

Journey for Maria

"Assunta, I tell you we'd do better to leave this place," Luigi exclaimed.

But the mother only bent over the fire and banked the embers. The flame glowed warmly. Their three children gathered about the hearth spread their hands to the heat. Assunta straightened up, heaved a sigh, but said nothing.

"You know, I was talking to the Cimarellis last night. They are leaving in the spring," he continued.

It was like a shock to her! Assunta guessed immediately that her husband had reached a decision with their neighbor. He was trying to break the news gently.

For several winters now the idea of immigrating had tempted him. Luigi was a hard working farmer, a man of action. On bad days when snow and rain confined him to pacing the kitchen from window to door, from door to cupboard and back again, he could not help complaining about the land and climate. It was useless to argue with him, thought Assunta. She had tried it often. Early she had learned that discussion was futile. So now she was ready to accept what she could not prevent. She fought back the tears.

"Then you wish that we leave with them?", she asked.

Her voice was calm and slow. Luigi looked at her, but her eyes remained fixed on the flames. She seemed resigned. He had not expected so easy a victory.

"Yes, Assunta, we must. We can no longer remain here. Over there you will be much happier, believe me. In the neighborhood of Rome there are vacant farms and lands to be leased. We will find ourselves something worth-while."

The storm-door slammed! A blizzard was at its height. Snow was falling heavily. Winters are severe in the neighborhood of Ancona and though one might well love that country for its pure air and steep pathways, when storms arise and fuel is low, it can become a land of misery.

There was a long silence in the Goretti home. The two boys and Maria continued to warm themselves by the fire. Assunta passed a damp cloth over the table she had just cleared.

She was a farm-bred, healthy woman, in her early thirties. Slender still in spite of the loose skirts that hung in folds about her. Luigi watched her work. Her slow movements spoke more eloquently than words of the painful fatigue and discouragement. He understood that she had just accepted the hardest sacrifice of her life. She was attached to this village, where she had always lived; where her parents lay buried. She had known no other horizon than these mountain slopes. With him it was different. As a soldier he had traveled over the Apennines and through the fertile plains beyond.

"Why should one kill oneself in these mountains steeped in rock, rubble, and harsh weather for reasons of sentiment?" He had asked himself time and time again.

The cold weather whistled under the door. The three youngsters were becoming sleepy by the hearth. Assunta was now washing the dishes. Luigi's anguish mounted. With his fingernail he scraped a hole in the frost on the windowpane. A huge blanket of white covered everything and the snow continued. There was no end of it. It was up to the height of the well now. The stone bench and the rose bushes were buried from sight.

Then a little hand slipped into his own. He lowered his eyes, and the hard lines in his face softened. It was his darling Maria who had come to press herself to his side. He kissed her forehead and ran his fingers through her long chestnut hair. This little girl of six was his favorite. She had indeed a temper that broke out occasionally, but in her calmer moments she was so affectionate and sweet! She turned her limpid eyes to her father and begged him to take her in his arms. Her rosy cheeks reminded Luigi of warmth and sunshine out beyond the Appennines on the shores of the Mediterranean.

Later when the children had been put to bed, Assunta and Luigi sat long before the fire and spoke in hushed voices. But Maria was listening. She heard them speak of a long journey, and her sleep was filled with marvelous dreams.

At length the winter passed. The snow melted and rivers rushed madly to the sea. Then one bright morning Luigi loaded his cart, hitched up his oxen and drove slowly away from Corinaldo. All he had left was his household goods and a few hundred lire, for he had sold his cottage and his field. The two boys Angelo and Marino, age nine and four, played amid the bundles of belongings. Assunta, sitting in front with Maria and Luigi, was nursing a new-born child, Allessandro.

The Cimarelli cart followed behind them. Domenico and Luigi had always been close neighbors. Theresa and Assunta, friends from childhood, would not have wished to be separated for anything in the world.

Together they crossed the Apennines. Together they followed the winding road toward Rome. It took them several weeks to make the two-hundred mile journey by ox cart. At times Luigi walked behind, deep in thought.

Maria watched the white mountain peaks fade in the distance. In her young mind was impressed forever that last picture—the great snowy heights of Corinaldo reaching heavenward.

2.

Home in the Swampland

They arrived at last. But Luigi soon began to think it were better had they never come!

For two days the Gorettis and Cimarellis wandered the streets of Rome. To these simple farmers, the great city was a universe. They knew not where to go, helplessly wandering about, retracing their steps. A dozen times they repassed the same place without noticing it. They visited Churches, prayed before the Virgin's statues, lit candles, called on the saints. Yet, despite the prayers, a pitiless fate seemed to steer them toward their ruin.

From a chance acquaintance they learned that Count Mazzoleni owned rich lands in the neighborhood of Nettuno. He rented them out, they were told, at a reasonable price. Or better still, he ceded them on a profit-sharing basis. They were supposed to be good farms, lands that furnished a rich livelihood regardless of the year. There were swamps there, too, and the climate was damp. But that should not stop anyone.

"Why not go there?" the stranger suggested "You can see for yourself. I know the place. It belongs to the district of Conca. Stop off at Ferriere and inquire. They'll tell you where it is."

Luigi and Domenico thanked the good man and set off without further delay. If only they had known what lay in store for them.

As they approached the marshes the air became heavy. Heavy, too, was the cart in which the children, tired of their cramped quarters, began to complain. Maria alone was patient and quiet. With her little legs hanging over the back of the cart, she thought on many things. The heavy wheels rumbled on the pavement. She was not worried or concerned about where this strange adventure would end, and it little mattered to her where they would be by dusk. She noted that they were leaving the city. Little by little all that great world was left behind—its many people, its beautiful Churches, its great houses stuck close one upon the other. Soon they were out in the open country, and vineyards and fields of wheat and corn appeared. It was hot and she was thirsty, but father had said there would be no stopping. The oxen trudged along. Luigi was whistling in contentment. Domenico cracked his whip.

When they saw afar off the first houses of Ferriere, they sighed with relief. The journey had been long. Luigi stood up and peered through the trees at a turn in the road. He noticed that there was no Church spire. But then you cannot expect everything. He urged on his beast and in short time they were in the midst of the poor village. No shops welcomed them. Not a door nor window was ajar along the dirty road. It was siesta time and apparently strictly observed. Luigi knocked three times at one of the houses. There was no reply but movements within gave hope of an answer. The door was unbolted, and a wrinkled old lady peered through the opening with blinding eyes.

"Could you tell me where to find Count Mazzoleni's farm?", Luigi asked.

The old woman was not quite awake, and it was necessary to repeat louder.

"Oh, you mean the old cheese factory!" She took a step forward in the doorway. "It's over there on your left. The last place, you can't miss it."

They found the place all right. It was an oblong, tile-roofed building set on a rise of ground. All about it was flat, low-lying, swampy farm. The children piled out of the cart and began exploring the yard. The heat was intense. There were no trees about the place, nor shade of any description. Everything seemed dead. The hen house was empty and the stone-watering-trough scorched and dry.

Luigi and Assunta looked over the farm,

visited the stable and shed, went through the kitchen and two rooms of the house, then climbed the stairway to the upper floor. They met neither dog nor cat, nor any other living thing. And thus without arousing anyone they took possession of Ferriere farm.

Next day the arrangements were settled. Luigi and Domenico became share-croppers of Count Mazzoleni. The Cimarellis took over the house adjacent to that of the Gorettis. They were not partners—just neighbors.

Assunta very quickly had the place cleaned and swept. Misery was stalking them but hope was adamant.

It was a dangerous situation for this family, accustomed to the invigorating air of the mountain heights to become stranded on the edge of the Pontine Marshes, which were damp and unhealthy, a hotbed of malaria.

But Luigi set about his work courageously. No longer was he working with little plots, one higher than the other, as at Corinaldo. Here low-lying fields and meadows stretched out in flat panorama.

For the past three years the property had been neglected. The preceding hired-man had lived on the spontaneous yield of the ground without taking any pains to develop its resources. Neglected ditches failed to carry off the excess water which spread out in pools over the land. With great energy Luigi tried to bring the land under control. Ditch digging occupied him for the rest of the summer. The water seeped off and plowing began. By fall he was able to sow eight acres in wheat and barley. But such rugged labor in the heat and damp of the Pontian Marshes was too much, even for the robust farmer of the mountain country. His strength was undermined.

The first attacks of fever were light, and he paid no attention to them. Assunta urged him to rest. But Luigi could not remain idle, and set out to work as though nothing were the matter. A few days later, coughing commenced and then he was obliged to admit his defeat. For a week he lay in bed suffering from bronchial trouble. But no sooner was he up again than he set about working on the roadway, and for two weeks hauled rocks and stone from the quarry. Then hedge trimming and fire-wood took up his attention. On through the winter he worked desperately in spite of continued weakness and a bothersome cough. As soon as the land was in shape, he undertook repair of the buildings. Repair of roofs, cleaning of lofts, partitions in the stable . . . one task followed another, one project gave rise to others. He went and came without rest; without thought of the dread disease that was undermining his health.

Meanwhile, in the home, Maria was maturing rapidly. Her little eyes were opening upon life, her little hands learning the family arts. Before too long death would come to pay a visit and hardship already hovered over Ferriere.

3.

Coming of the Serenellis

Harvest time came. Luigi sharpened his sickle and set out early. He was counting on doing it alone. If he hired no one to help bring in the crop, there would be more sustenance for his family. That was his last imprudence.

In the first days all went well. The sheaves, accumulating behind him, lent ardor to his task. For hours at a time he bent over the furrows, dripping with sweat, not pausing an instant. It was foolish for him to work so hard. Each evening he came back more worn out than the preceding day. He went to bed with hardly any supper. At this rate he could not carry on. Toward the end of the week he became dizzy and one whole afternoon he lay helpless in the field. When he finally struggled back to the house, he was breathing heavily.

The next morning he was unable to go to Sunday Mass at Campo Morto. Monday he was prostrate in bed, unable even to think of returning to work. That same morning Count Mazzoleni came to examine his Ferriere farm. He was quite dismayed to see Luigi's harvest delayed more than that of his neighbors. Their crops were practically in the barn, while Luigi's crops, half-mowed, lay limp upon the field. The grain was over-ripe and any day it might fall. The Count could not understand why the bundles had not been gathered up. Luigi was apparently lying down on the job. Mazzoleni was quite angry and resolved to let his hired man know his mind. He stormed into the house and vent his wrath upon the helpless invalid.

Luigi knew not what to reply. He tried to explain and finished by admitting that he would not be able to bring in the harvest. He would have to have help, at least for a time. After that he would be able to maintain the farm.

"I'll send you two men tomorrow," Count Mazzoleni cut in. "The harvest can't wait any longer! Giovanni Serenilli and his son came to me this morning looking for work. I'll send them to you, and you can make your own arrangements."

Luigi remained silent. His weakness and the thought of having to share the fruits of his labors was heavy upon him. Whatever the price, there was no other solution. It remained to be seen how Assunta would take it. He called his wife and decided to tell her, but then his courage failed him. She, too, was overburdened with work. A few weeks ago she had given birth to Ersilia and was too occupied with the children even to sit down for supper. Luigi watched her straighten up the sick-room and kept silent. He realized how two more men in the house would be a terrible burden on her. She certainly would not agree to lodge and feed them.

Slowly plans turned about in his mind. He could lend them his ox-cart to take them to Nettuno each evening and back again in the morning. Or, again, he might find them lodging in the village somewhere. But each idea was so impractical —lack of time, lack of lodging. Besides he was not able to hire them at a fixed salary. He had not fifty lire to his name. Of necessity he must take them into partnership and cede them part of the house. Then another series of insurmountable difficulties crowded in upon him.

Luigi was not well and his troubles wore him down. When the children were asleep, Assunta returned. The husband and wife said their evening prayers together and put out the light. "Tomorrow." Luigi thought, "I'll tell her", and made a great effort to lose his troubles in sleep.

Giovanni Serenelli and his son knocked on the door early next morning and introduced themselves in the provincial speech of Ancona. Surprise and embarrassment yielded to the tale of hardship and want. At first, Assunta did not understand the object of their visit. As she dressed the children in the bedroom she followed the conversation in the kitchen. They spoke in her native dialect and of persons and places that were dear to her. Giovanni seemed to be about sixty. He had an easy flow of speech and knew how to touch Luigi with the recital of his miseries. His wife had died in an insane asylum. Another son was still there. The other children were married and settled in the region about Ancona. He was left alone and penniless with this youngest son, Alexander. Luigi looked at the young man. He was well-built and apparently strong beyond his eighteen years.

At length they came to the vital question. Giovanni proposed sharing work and profits on a fifty-fifty basis. "Count Mazzoleni," he said, "proposed that arrangement yesterday evening. Besides, we don't need much in the way of lodging. We can all eat together and we'll get along fine."

Old Serenelli was very amicable and would not hear of detailed conditions. What he wanted most, he said, was a home and family life; he had suffered enough loneliness since the death of his wife.

Luigi was touched with sympathy and gave in. Even Assunta did not dare interfere. The deal was concluded and the newcomers began work immediately.

The following Monday Luigi accompanied Giovanni and his son to Nettuno to get their furniture and belongings. The trio returned together. Two iron beds were set up in a room Assunta had prepared. Their meatloaf and bread were put in the cupboard with the Goretti food supply. Their clothing was hung in the family press. In the evening they supped together. The common life had begun.

4.

Misunderstanding and Warning

For the first few days, even the first weeks, all went well in the Goretti home. It is rather easy to get along with those who come from one's own native place and speak one's own dialect. Giovanni and Alexander were out to work early—the harvest was under control. Assunta prepared her best meals. The children were happy and after work-hours played with the new boy. He taught them how to catch birds. He could make reed whistles. They were fascinated by the things he could do. A bit of joy returned to the Goretti household. Hope lighted again. The sheaves of wheat piled up in the barn. "Better days are coming," thought Luigi.

As long as the heavy work lasted there was no misunderstanding or discussion. The newcomers were hard workers. They lost no time, and in the evening they were too tired to wrangle. After the harvest, the sale of the produce and the plowing kept them busy.

Then winter set in, with its long days of rain and idleness. Time hung on their hands. Old Serenelli took to drinking. The habit that poverty had driven out reasserted itself. The wine of those southern lands is strong and though he rarely became drunk, his character soured. He was irritable, overbearing, and dissatisfied.

Alexander, too, began to show evil tendencies. Having lost his mother in childhood, there was a void in his heart. He resented the fact that he had been left to the careless tutelage of a cousin —then to an aunt. His own father had taken no interest in him. At the age of twelve, he had found work with the stevedores. In that first apprenticeship he had learned the foulest language of the sea, and would curse and swear on the least provocation. At fifteen he led a lonely life. His character was warped, and the family life at Ferriere could not alter it.

He became increasingly taciturn, shunned the children, had no friends, and visited no one. When the others went to Mass at Nettuno or Campo Morto, he went off by himself. Assunta noted that he went regularly to a news-stand, and came back with a bundle of lurid magazines. He would then lock himself in his room and would not come out for the rest of the day. This brooding had an evil effect on him. His manner darkened and something of the sneak appeared in his look. Assunta became alarmed. She wondered what was going on in his soul . . . and soon, to her grief she would learn.

The next time Assunta cleaned Alexander's room she saw with dismay that he had clipped a number of immodest pictures from the magazines, and hung them about his bed. Her first impulse was to seize them and put them in the fire. But she refrained. That would only start a quarrel and bring more trouble into the home. Perhaps it would be better not to interfere. She was not, after all, responsible for his conduct. His father knew of these things and it was up to him to take action. But she resolved to watch over her eldest, Angelo. He was approaching his teens and the evil influence of a good-for-nothing might lead him astray. She forbade him strictly to enter the Serenelli room. She did not breathe a word, even to Luigi, of her discovery.

Things went from bad to worse. Luigi suspected that Giovanni was slyly disposing of grain from their common store. That needed to be settled. He proposed separation in equal lots of the produce. The terms of agreement between friends would have to be made practical. Giovanni became exacting. There was quarreling and harsh words. It might have gone to blows if Luigi had not ceded for the sake of peace in the home.

The poor man sighed for his mountain home. He regretted especially having admitted these two men to his fellowship. If he could only stand up against them and maintain his paternal authority! But he felt weak in the face of them and capitulated. Malaria had undermined his strength, and during the winter it accomplished its work.

By spring a subtle apathy laid hold of him. Chills came and went at intervals, but he held on stubbornly. He tried not to complain and went out to work with apparently the same ardor, only he never seemed to urge on his oxen as before. In the evening he sat down as soon as he entered the house, but ate very little. Assunta noted his exhaustion, his palid complexion, and the dark circles under his eyes, but what was to be done? she dared not say anything. The contract to work must be kept.

Toward the end of April he went to bed. The sickness was making great strides. Maria ran over to Nettuno for quinine, but it brought little relief. In less than ten days Luigi's strength was gone. His breathing was quick and measured. His pale arms lay limp on the covers. The little children, without too well understanding the significance, knelt about the bed in prayer. Maria especially, his own little Maria, redoubled her fervent prayers and wept in silence.

One afternoon Luigi had a spasm of suffocation. He threw his head back and remained still, his hands tense. Assunta was alarmed. Giovanni and Alexander were out in the fields. She sent Maria in haste to get help. The little girl hurried out and notified all the neighbors. When she got back Luigi had regained consciousness. She went

MISUNDERSTANDING AND WARNING

over to his bed. A smile of tenderness played about his lips, and with his icy hand he touched the moist forehead of his darling.

"How warm you are, Maria, where have you been?" The little girl hesitated a moment and then whispered:

"It is nothing, papa, I just ran in from outside." And she took the trembling hand of her father in her own little warm hands and kissed it.

A few days later Luigi asked for the priest. This was journey's end. The neighbors assembled silently in the room of the dying man. Assunta had placed a crucifix and two candles on the white covering of a little table. Holy water and a twig were there too, with a few pieces of cotton. All knelt to recite the rosary while waiting for the priest. Luigi followed the prayers. His lips moved and he tried to answer. Then he drifted off in sleep, and in his last dream memories returned.

He saw again the low cottages of Corinaldo with their red tile roofs on the mountain slope. He saw the lofty bell-tower from where the Adriatic was visible. Wind whistled through the valley and shook the olive trees. Sheets were spread beneath the branches to catch the precious fruit. The oil-press turned in the yard. Again he climbed the pathway to his field, but it was much steeper now and his breath came short. Pictures became jumbled in his imagination.

He opened his eyes. The candles were lit. He looked about at all the neighbors praying. He seemed to be looking for someone. All were hushed in silence. Finally his gaze set, the eyes of a dying man, glowing like embers on the hearth of a darkened room. Giovanni and Alexander were standing there in the doorway.

Luigi wanted to cry out but was unable to. He tried to rise but fell back on the pillow. Assunta leaned over him. He murmured in a broken voice that only she could hear. "Assunta . . . go back . . . to Corinaldo."

When the priest came Luigi was breathing lightly, but he was still fully conscious. They were left alone. Then he received the last Sacraments and answered to the Last Blessing. He seemed more calm now. Yet from time to time he raised himself and repeated with suppliant haggard eyes: "Assunta . . . go back to Corinaldo . . . go back to Corinaldo."

Some thought he was delirious. That same evening he died.

5.

Maria's Happiest Day

"Mother, when will I make my First Communion? I can no longer live without Jesus."

It was the month of June, 1901. Maria Goretti would soon be eleven. At that time it was not customary to receive before twelve, except in rare cases. God knows with what ardour the lovely girl longed for that happy day. Divine grace was working within her soul with such strength that it had already aroused an insatiable hunger for the Holy Eucharist.

"Your First Communion? But, my child," replied the mother sadly, "how can you do it? You can't read . . . and I have nothing to pay for your dress and slippers. We have no time to spare; there is so much work to be done here."

"At that rate I can never make my First Communion," Maria pleaded, "and I want Jesus so badly."

"What can your poor mother do? It hurts me to see you grow up without instruction, like the animals of the field."

"Well, mother, if that is the case, don't worry. God will see to it. There is a lady at Conca, Elvira Schiassi, who can read. I will hurry through the housework, if you will let me go to Conca to learn the Catechism. Besides Dom Paliana comes from Citerna every Sunday to teach religion. He will instruct me with the other children preparing for First Communion."

The mother consented to the proposal, and for eleven months Maria prepared for that great moment when Jesus would come to her as the Bread of Life. Her First Communion was a triumph of her tenacious piety over the rather rigid piety of her mother. Without that tenacity and constancy she would have died probably without ever having received.

Once the decision was made, Assunta saw to it that her daughter received instruction. Sometimes she took Maria to Campo Morto or to Conca. Again she would send Maria to the Passionist Fathers at Nettuno that she might learn to go to Confession and prepare for Holy Communion. As the great day approached, Assunta began to wonder if her daughter was really ready? Did she understand the act she was about to perform? Poor Assunta was troubled with anxieties and responsibilities for her Maria. Finally, she set the matter

MARIA'S HAPPIEST DAY

before Dom Temistocle Signori, the Archpriest of Nettuno.

The wise and holy Dom Signori examined the girl and filled with the admiration at her answers expressed his complete satisfaction. "Be at ease, good mother. Your daughter is very well prepared. Put away all your vain fears and confide her to Mary Immaculate. Place her under the Virgin's protecting mantle and have no fear."

Assunta followed the priest's advice, and years later she was able to say: "My Maria made her First Communion like a saint."

From that day Maria intensified her piety and recollection, her obedience to her mother, and her care of brothers and sisters. Playthings and nice clothes had no interest for her. She was busy preparing her soul for her Jesus. One day she returned home beaming. "Mamma mia! Dom Signori said I would make my First Communion on the Feast of Corpus Christi."

All Ferriere hamlet had part in her adornment for that great event. One furnished slippers, another the veil, a third a crown of flowers. Assunta offered her own earrings to enhance the beauty of her daughter. Maria was wrapped in expectation. With tears of joy and compunction she knelt before her mother, her brothers, her sisters, and her neighbors, to ask pardon of her faults.

Twelve other girls and two boys composed the First Communion class. A Passionist, Father Jerome, from the Retreat of Our Lady of Grace at Nettuno, was the celebrant of the Mass. During the sermon he addressed the children with fervent words on the great love of Jesus for them. He exhorted them warmly ever to preserve their souls pure and innocent, and *to die rather than commit a mortal sin.* He recommended to them the practice of saying three Hail Marys each evening in honor of Mary Immaculate.

These warm exhortations added fuel to the already growing flame of love in the heart of Maria. What were her words of love to Jesus? What did the Divine Host say to her at this great tryst of two inflamed hearts? The glow of her countenance, the modesty and gravity of her bearing, showed only a feeble glimmer of the Light that burned within. While the other children hastened to the sacristy after Mass to thank Father Jerome, Maria remained behind, wrapped in a silent intimate colloquy with her God.

A light cloud of sadness veiled the complete joy of this day . . . the remembrance of her dead father. Maria loved her hard working father, as only an eldest daughter of the poor can love her parent. The hardships of his life were ever present to her mind. His great sacrifice and pain at having to quit this life before having provided for his family were deeply impressed on her memory. Each evening before retiring to rest, she had said the entire rosary for the repose of his soul. Whenever she had passed by the cemetry where he lay, she paused to say a Hail Mary for him. And now while furtive tears stole down her cheeks, from her heart a fervent prayer went heavenward for her dear father.

Throughout the whole day Maria remained under the spell of the Princely visit of that morning. A visible joy beamed in her countenance and colored all her words and actions. Maria, ever docile and obliging, now became ardent in her endeavor to serve and to please. The good Assunta took the occasion to urge on her daughter: "You have received Jesus today. You must try ever so hard now to be good and pleasing to Him." Toward evening Maria's thoughts started in a new direction. "Oh! when shall I be able to receive Jesus again?"

So ended the happiest day of her life. The King of Martyrs had come to nourish with His own Body and Blood this lily of purity, and the day was not far distant when He would come again and take her home with Him.

6.

The Little Woman

Time passed over the grave of Luigi. Life at Ferriere became very sad. Assunta experienced many an hour of deep distress. She had hoped at first to be able to return to her native village. Deep down she had long been homesick, and besides it was the last wish of her poor Luigi. But it was necessary to set aside this dream. How could she with neither money nor assistance undertake such a journey with her children? Angelo, her eldest, was scarcely thirteen. So she resigned herself to remaining at Ferriere, where Giovanni had become master. He was harsh and would not even accept her for work in the fields except on the condition that Maria, now going on twelve, take her place in the house.

Maria had become one of those children whom

hardship and bitter experience of life make serious beyond their years. She went about her chores with scarcely a smile on her face, a bit of sadness in her deep brown eyes. Overnight she had changed from a laughing girl to a quiet little woman, preoccupied with her responsibilities.

Now Maria must manage the household and care for her little brothers and sisters. Meals, washing and mending occupied her from early morning to late at night. At any hour of the day she could be seen working about the kitchen, her long chestnut hair curling over her shoulders. It was her pleasure to be helpful, obedient, and obliging. If, at times, she paused at the door and gazed dreamily at the distant horizon, it was because the first troublesome moods of adolescence were stealing over her.

She was tall for her age. One would have taken Maria to be fourteen or fifteen. She was slender and graceful and with the black shawl over her shoulders, she looked more like the young lady of tomorrow. But her soul was at peace and quickly she took up each duty.

Unfortunately Maria had never gone to school. She knew not how to read nor write. Like her mother before her, she was a poor unlettered country girl. Her prayers she learned by heart from Assunta, and now, in turn, she was teaching them to her brothers and sisters. When she made her First Communion, she was behind the others. To be the poorest, the most humble, was her lot in life. She did not realize, though, that she was also the richest in virtue and most loved by Him who that day had given Himself to her.

Soon that great day was slipping into memory and it seemed as though Maria would be lost in the obscurity of the swampland. For God had chosen her to do great early deeds. She heard no mysterious voices, like Joan calling her to feats of battle. The bread she gave to the poor did not turn to roses in her apron, as with Germaine. Unlike Bernadette and Therese, Our Lady did not smile on her. Maria expected nothing. Between her morning prayer and her nightly remembrance of her Father, she did only the holy will of God.

One morning not long after her First Communion, Maria had gone down to the public well in Ferriere to draw water. While waiting for her bucket to fill, she had overheard one of the village girls telling her boy-friend an off-color joke. Maria recognized this girl as one of her companions in the First Communion class . . . and was shocked. "How could she so soon forget Jesus?"

Hurrying home, Maria could not contain herself. Hardly was she in the door when the words tumbled out in a torrent: "Mama! Do you know . . . at the well . . . the girl said terrible things . . . and the boy laughed . . ."

"Why then did you listen?" chided her mother.

"I couldn't help it! I had to wait for the bucket to fill."

"Yes," Assunta nodded wisely. "I know you are astonished that girls and boys talk about such things. Just remember, if you were to say such things, people would be even more astonished at you."

Maria could hardly believe her ears. Did her mother really think that she would ever offend God in that dreadful way? "Talk about such things," she said with amazement in her voice, "why I would rather die . . ."

But all was not serious. At rare intervals there were innocent distractions in her life. On those days with her godmother and neighbor, Theresa Cimarelli, she went to market at Nettuno to sell vegetables and eggs. Maria enjoyed those seven miles of pleasant talk, while their cart jogged along and the pigeons cooed in their cages. She who was so silent, now had much to say. Maria at these times refound her childhood gaiety.

Unfortunately, these hours of fun were few and passed all too quickly. Tomorrow she would take up her daily routine again. Tomorrow she would muster her courage and begin anew, without complaint, the same old tasks.

Little did this girl realize the way that God was leading her . . . and that on one of those tomorrows she would need the strength of a martyr!

7.

The Angel of Darkness

It was getting close to the end of June. The day had been very sultry and now with the night there was a bit of cool air creeping up from the swamps. Toads and frogs could be heard croaking for rain, while a hoot-owl, nestled in the hollow of an old elm, was sending forth his stupid wail into the night.

At Ferriere behind closed doors the kitchen fire smouldered to ashes. All was wrapped in sleep save the white form at the bedside.

Maria had not gone to rest. Kneeling in her night gown for evening prayer, she seemed to continue indefinitely. At the examination of conscience she had faltered and knew not how to continue. Strange things that day had upset her soul. Examination of conscience, ordinarily so easy and rapid, now became painful and complicated. There were things that she did not well understand. An evil she could only guess and yet not know, troubled her conscience. She was filled with shame and deep trouble and wondered if she had offended her God. Thoughts of Alexander, too, frightened her.

And now, before God she recalls everything that happened. One day last week her mother had been too tired to work and had remained at home. She had sent Maria to take her place in the fields. It was a pleasure for the girl to help and she had set out with Alexander to hoe at the other end of the property. They were alone in the field now, working side by side for more than an hour. Suddenly Alexander, throwing aside his hoe, crossed the furrow that separated them, and stood before her.

He seemed beside himself. His eyes were alight with a strange fire. He seized Maria by the arms, stammering words that she could not grasp. She was stupified, unable to understand what he wanted. Then it suddenly dawned on her that he was soliciting her to sin. Indignation brought the blood to her face. Violently she shook herself free and fled down the field. She hid herself in a hedge till noon, and then went in for lunch. In the afternoon she pretended to return to work with him, but under the pretext of getting a basket in the barn, had climbed to the loft and buried herself in the hay, where she remained motionless for three hours.

Thus for a whole week she had avoided him. Never would she let herself be caught alone with him. She seemed confident he would not try again.

But this morning he had surprised her. She had been making the beds. There was no one in the house. He had entered from behind and taken hold of her. She had sunk her nails into his face until he cursed in pain and let her go. Immediately she had started for the door to call for help, but he was there before her and silenced her with a threat:

"If you say a word to your mother, I'll kill you." And he shook his fist before her frightened eyes.

Alexander had gone out and she had locked herself in her own room. She feared he might return and so was afraid even to go to the kitchen to prepare the meal. When, through the window, she saw her mother returning from work, she hurried to start the fire. But it was too late. The soup was not warm by noon and she had not had time to set the table. She received a harsh scolding. Alexander, seated before an empty plate, laughed and made sport of her.

How it pained her! Once she thought she would tell all. The words were there on her tongue, but she bit her lips. What was the use? Her poor mother could do nothing. And if the evil intentions of Alexander were known there would be more wranglings with the Serenellis. Life would become unbearable. Then, too, he had said he would kill her. It would be best to keep her secret to herself.

But tonight at her bedside, reliving the painful hours of this sad day she was unable to keep back her tears. Her little body trembled and a wave of fear swept over her. Her throat was dry and tense. She buried her head in the covers and her prayer terminated in bitter sobs.

This was not a childish vexation. From now on the soul of Maria is different. A veil of sadness clouds her eyes. Her smile is gone. There is nothing left of the little girl, neither laughter nor the playfulness that at times betrayed her eleven years. She understands at last. Her actions are measured, her words are rare. She avoids sitting down at the common table and flees Alexander as one might flee a plague.

But he seeks her out, as she well perceives. He waits, he watches, he follows her about the house. The cat and mouse story has begun. It is a duel unsuspected even by Assunta. Maria becomes increasingly reticent. The terrible threat rings in her ears and each time she sees Alexander she reads in his eyes: "If you speak, I'll kill you."

From now on Maria lives under a reign of terror. Formerly, when she was small, the ghost-stories of her father did not even frighten her; she laughed heartily at them. When she was eight she was not afraid to cross the yard in blackest night to shut the door of the hen house. And on the way to Mass at Conca she would run ahead of the rest to beat off the snakes that lay in their path.

She could not remember ever having been afraid. But now, whenever she is alone, an indefinable anguish chills her heart. Alexander might come back. Alexander might surprise her. Alexander might overcome her. She feels so weak.

But no. A voice in prayer reassures her and tells her she is strong.

Who shall be able to overcome God living in her heart?

8.

Even to Blood

It is once more high noon. The sun from its zenith beats down on the Ferriere farm. A burning wind, stormladen, sweeps across the swamps, licks the walls of the house and enters the kitchen by the open door.

The Gorettis and Serenellis as usual are seated about the table. They have just finished their lunch. It is so hot that they delay a bit before returning to work. If Giovanni would permit, they would gladly take their siesta. But he insists on working immediately after lunch and they await his orders. Maria is doing dishes, amidst a silence broken only by the clatter of the plates.

Hay and straw are already in the barn, but the unthrashed beans are still spread out in the yard, drying in the sun.

"Go harness the team!" Giovanni orders. "There is no time to lose! We will have rain this afternoon. The beans will have to be in beforehand."

Slowly Alexander and Angelo rise. Assunta clears the table and pushes the benches beneath it. The other children scamper out of doors. Giovanni alone does not move. "Put the beans in bags and take them up to the loft!", he continues.

But Alexander does not hear his father. He has another project in mind. For the past hour his eyes have followed Maria. Before returning to work, he goes to his room where he is heard fumbling in his closet.

"Maria, I have a torn shirt that needs mending," he calls out. "I'll need it to go to Mass tomorrow. You'll have to repair it for me this afternoon. I'm leaving it for you on my bed." And this he says with studied nonchalance.

The dishwashing stopped, but there was no reply. Within the girl's heart emotions struggled for expression. She felt like crying: "No! I have no time . . ." and it would have relieved her. But in spite of an instinctive repugnance to do this, she consented again to be of service. True charity won out in her heart.

While he was harnessing the oxen in the stable, Alexander's thoughts pursued their evil trend. His plans took definite shape. He visualized the scene. Maria will be quietly seated by the bed, and there will be nobody in the house but the baby, Theresa. He will hurry in, close the kitchen door, then lock the door of his room. It will be so easy!

"Giddap!" he calls to the oxen. Then leaping on the cart he drives out into the yard.

For want of a thrasher, the Gorettis improvised a method of their own. The beanstalks were heaped in the yard and the cart loaded with youngsters passed and repassed over the piles. Meanwhile, Assunta turned and shook the lot with her fork.

Poor mother, her heart was full as she paused from time to time to witness the joy of her little ones. "Look at Angelo," she muses, "so like his father directing the cart. What a consolation he is to me—my eldest. If we can only carry on for a little while longer, perhaps things will be brighter. Then, too, there's my Maria, so good to everyone! She is so sweet and holy. Maybe she's a little to reserved. For the past month—especially since her First Communion—she seems to be timid and worried. She hardly speaks and her eyes are always downcast. She blushes so easily—her prayers are prolonged. What can be taking place in her soul? Apparently she has some secret . . . but then she is at that age when girls are easily disturbed."

Thus while the oxen turn on the thrashing floor and the children shout and laugh, Assunta pursues the thread of her maternal love—her only joy on earth. Suddenly Alexander stops the cart and jumps down. "Take my place for a while," he tells Assunta, "I forgot my handkerchief in my room. I'll be right back." His forehead is moist with sweat.

Obediently Assunta puts aside her fork and climbs up in his place. The cart is off again and the joy of children and mother is doubled.

Then as Alexander disappears through the doorway, a flash of lightning is seen on the horizon and a clap of thunder follows. The storm is approaching. The noon-day devil prowls about the Ferriere farm.

Meanwhile, Maria is seated on the porch above the kitchen door. It is much too hot within the house. She has taken Alexander's shirt and found a whole sleeve torn. It will be a long job, but courageously she sets about it and her needle flies to and fro. Beside her on a blanket her baby sister, Theresa, is fast asleep. From the other side of the house comes hardly a sound to disturb her of contentment and hope. Alone she dreams of the morrow.

"Tomorrow will be Sunday, feast of the Precious Blood. I will start early with Theresa Cimarelli," she tells herself, "so we can get to Confession and Communion."

Her little soul expands already in anticipation. She has so much to tell, so much advice to seek, such great strength to receive.

Suddenly Alexander looks out of the kitchen door. She jumps with apprehension. He has seen her on the porch. Up the stairway he comes and without a word passes into the bedroom. Why has he come? She can hear him fumbling with tools in the end room. What is he up to? Perhaps he forgot to take a sickle with him. Then he reappears in the doorway.

"Maria, come here!"

His voice is harsh, and she is thoroughly frightened. The sewing drops to her lap and she neither answers nor moves.

"Hear me! Come here immediately!" Alexander is already very impatient. He grabs her by the arm and though she clings to the banister and calls for help, it is of no avail. He drags her roughly into the room and bolts the door. She is his prisoner with little chance of escape. The bird is caught and a fiendish grin curls his lips.

Only too well does she understand his intention. But in spite of the frightened sobs that climb in her throat, a supernatural energy animates her. She will defend herself to the end—even to death if need be.

"Give in, Maria. Let me have you, or else . . .", and he holds up a knife threateningly.

Frantically Maria wrenches free and screams for help . . . but who can hear amid the noise of the cart and children and beans. She leaps around the table for protection, but with a laugh he knocks it aside and trips her. As she falls he pins her down with his knee.

"I'll not take NO for an answer," he snarls. "Are you going to give in or must I kill you?"

Her only reply is a wild struggle for release, twisting and scratching and biting.

"No! No! I will not! I will not!"

Alexander had not expected such resistance. Apparently she will not consent. "Why?" he argues, "Why will you not?"

"Because it is a sin. God forbids it. You will go to hell, Alexander. You will go to hell if you do it."

Her constancy seems only to enrage him. But he knows how to quiet her. He draws the cruel knife menacingly over her and asks for the last time:

"Will you, or will you not?"

For an instant Maria is quiet. She knows the danger. This brute that is crushing her with his weight is now capable of anything. He is getting beside himself with rage. His eyes are blood-shot.

She pleads desperately: "Alexander, let me go! Let me go!"

The knife now hangs over her breast. She must choose: death or life, heaven or hell, God or Satan, sin or martyrdom. Then, is a burst of heroism, making desperate efforts to free herself, she chose energetically, superhumanly.

"No! I will not, Alexander, no!"

The tragedy followed. The infuriated Alexander says that something seemed to snap within him. With mad rage he plunged the steel into her breast and abdomen fourteen times.

"It was just like I was sticking a knife into a log," he testified later.

Maria uttered not a cry. She did not even attempt to ward off the blows. With her right hand she tried to hold her dress modestly over her knees. Then mercifully she lost consciousness.

Alexander thought her dead. Dumbfounded

he got up. Blood had sobered him. He threw the knife behind the closet, went to his own room, and locked the door.

The sun was now flooding in by the window. The black clouds were scattering in the distance; the storm had passed. The cracking of bean stalks and the shouts of the children continued in the yard.

9.

Hours of Pain

For another hour the thrashing carried on without respite, though less hurriedly, as the threatening storm had passed. All that remained was to separate the chaff from the grain and gather the precious harvest into the barn. In the evening a bonfire of stalks would symbolize the family joy and abundance.

But Alexander had not returned, baby Theresa was crying on the porch, and Assunta became worried.

"Mariano, go see what is keeping Alexander; and tell Maria to look after the baby. I'm afraid the child will fall down the stairs."

Suddenly a call resounded from the house. "Assunta! Assunta! Come here!" It was Giovanni, yelling as though the house were afire. What now? Surely something serious had happened.

The poor mother dropped everything and hurried up the stairs and into the room where Maria lay writhing in pain, close at her heels came her neighbors, Theresa Cimarelli and faithful Domenico. All were filled with confusion at the sight of Maria's bloody body and the room in disarray. Tenderly Domenico lifted Maria and carried her into the bedroom. The sight of the limp form of her daughter was too much for poor Assunta. She grew weak and fell fainting on the floor.

When Assunta revived, Theresa was working over Maria and Giovanni was explaining his story: "I was sleeping in the shade beside the house when the baby awoke me with her crying. I didn't pay much attention to that, but then I heard Maria calling with a feeble voice from the doorway. So I got up, and just in time to see her fall in the doorway. She had fainted, so I shouted for Assunta and all of you. I don't know what happened. But look, her dress is blood-stained."

Assunta leaned over her daughter: "What's the matter, Maria, did you hurt yourself?"

The girl made no reply. Apparently she was suffocating. With her hands she was trying to undo her clothing. Her mother lent a hand, unhooking and loosening the blouse, and a trickle of red blood crept across her throat. With infinite precaution the two women raised her a bit and slid out her arms from the sleeves, and removed the blouse. Her underclothing was all saturated with blood. The underwear, sticking to the wounds, had to be cut off bit by bit.

On her breast near the heart the thin blade had made a narrow but deep entry. Four gashes criss-crossed the stomach. The whole of that little body was horribly torn. Blood congealed about the wounds and trickled in drops upon the sheet.

The heroic child did not even whimper. It was her rest after the battle, repose after victory. Her long disheveled hair formed an aureole beneath her head. Her discolored lips remained closed. They had not yet revealed the name of the assailant.

"Maria, my little one, tell me what has happened? Who did this to you?"

Maria hesitated a bit, then raising her large innocent eyes to her mother she whispered: "It was Alexander, Mama."

"Who? Alexander! But why?"

Maria seemed to reflect before speaking. The whole drama repassed swiftly before her eyes. Then quietly she answered: "Because he wanted to commit an awful sin and I would not."

There was the secret of her martyrdom. The two women dared not pry further.

Meanwhile there was much going on outside. Domenico had hitched up his cart and had hurried off to get a doctor at Nettuno. Along the way he notified neighbors, and the tragic news flew from farm to farm. "A crime committed at Ferriere; Maria attacked."

Housework, plowing, gardens and sheep were abandoned, and the whole countryside seemed to flock to "the old cheese factory." Some of the men carried pitchforks, others staves and clubs, and still others came with rifles. No one knew what to expect.

Soon the house was thronged. Women were getting in each other's way and everybody wanted to see the little victim. She was so sweet and good! Some wept, others whispered in little groups. With each newcomer the details were told again and Alexander's name was repeated over and over. The blood on the floor seemed to tell its own story.

Suddenly there was a commotion. Someone discovered the knife behind the closet. Indignation flared up, tempers grew hot. "Alexander!" "Where is Alexander?"

He must be here," shouted one of the men trying the door. "But the door is barred from the inside." Several tried to force the oak panel with their shoulders. Someone suggested getting a crow-bar. Then Count Mazzoleni came rushing in. Seeing the men struggling to get at Alexander, he tried to calm them:

"No, wait, better notify the police. They'll come and arrest him." For Mazzoleni feared that these excited men might only add murder to murder. So two of the farmers then rushed off for the police—one to Nettuno and the other to Citerna.

But so many people and such turmoil in the next room was fatiguing to Maria. In vain did she beg to be left alone with her mother and godmother. Each one thought his or her presence necessary in the room . . Only Dr. Bartoli's arrival restored order and everyone was put out of the house.

The doctor made his examination quickly. The case was most serious. An operation was necessary. Another messenger was sent for an ambulance to bring Maria to the hospital. First aid was administered and with the help of bed-sheeting the little body was bandaged temporarily. Precious time slipped by in waiting for the ambulance and though the others were impatient, Maria alone remained quiet. Her little body was weakening steadily. Since two o'clock that afternoon she had been bleeding and it was six o'clock before the horse-drawn ambulance arrived.

10.

The Final Struggle

The stretcher had to be brought right up to the bedside. Maria had become limp. Painful gasps escaped her when the doctor and Domenico roused her, though they were ever so gentle. They laid her on the stretcher, covered her with a blanket, and carried her down to the ambulance at the bottom of the stairway.

Neighbors crowded around to see their Maria for the last time. Her brothers and sisters climbed into the wagon to kiss her good-bye. She was haggard, pale and disfigured. Tears welled up in her dark eyes and stole furtively down her cheeks. Assunta took her position at her head; the doctor sat up with the driver, and they were off. This was Maria's farewell to Ferriere . . . and theirs to her.

White pigeons careened overhead turning and fluttering about the roof she called home.

Many a time Maria had traveled these seven miles of dusty road to Nettuno. Many happy trips she had made along this way with Theresa Cimarelli to sell their poultry and eggs. Other times, too, she had gone this way with her dear mother to visit the shrine of Our Lady of Grace. She had been able to laugh then and enjoy life, which seemed pleasant in spite of hardships. But now her teeth are clenched, her face is set, and her hands clutch the side of the stretcher. The road is rough, the horses unsteady, and with every jolt her whole body is dipped anew in a flood of pain.

"Are you suffering, my little one?", Assunta asks.

Maria makes an effort to smile. "Yes, mama, a little. Have we still far to go?"

With great effort she turns her head a little to the side, trying to recognize some familiar landmark; trees along the way, the cemetery fence, the iron cross at the fork in the road. At last they reach the bridge over the canal—the halfway mark. How long these seven miles seem! Pain racks her body. Even breathing is painful. Stiffly her head returns on the cushion, her feverish eyes stare up into the blue heaven which never seemed so beautiful as now.

At a bend in the road two mounted policemen hurried past the ambulance. Between their two horses a handcuffed man was dragged on foot. Assunta was not able to conceal her surprise. In

THE FINAL STRUGGLE

the perspiring, dust-covered runner she recognized Alexander. Fortunately Maria had seen nothing.

As they entered Nettuno, crowds gathered and escorted the ambulance. The sad story had preceded them. The arrival of the criminal had been witnessed at the prison gates with threatening tumult. At the Orsenigo Hospital doorway throngs gathered in silent awe. Everybody wanted to see the heroine. And they did see her as the stretcher was borne up the stairway. Buried in a wave of chestnut hair, a beautiful, innocent face looked kindly out on them and tried to smile. When the doors of the Hospital shut her from their eyes, the crowd dispersed and some were heard to murmur: "She's a real martyr." The voice of the people had already canonized Maria Goretti.

Yet she had not achieved her full measure of suffering. A second time she must experience the knife on her flesh. The hospital chaplain came to visit her on the operating table. She betrayed no concern, but gladly went to Confession. She scarcely believed death to be near. At such an early age one does not feel death's approach. The body is too well equipped for reaction against even the most severe suffering. As the priest was leaving, a surgeon whispered in his ear: "Where you have found an angel I am afraid we will leave but a corpse."

Fourteen wounds were discovered, the intestines were torn, lungs were pierced completely through, and the heart grazed. The lower bone structure was seriously injured showing four chest wounds and five in the abdominal region. Added to this were five minor gashes. Stitching and bandaging only added torture to the poor sufferer. In spite of her intense pain, she uttered not a sound. She had no more strength left. The surgical work continued for two long hours. No anesthetic was administered because the attendants feared peritonitis. Finally she lost consciousness.

When Assunta entered the sick-room she thought her child was dead and she began to cry. Little by little Maria recovered. Her eyelids slowly opened. She called for water, but that little relief must be denied her, she willingly accepted the sacrifice in remembrance of Jesus' thirst on the Cross. She was told not to speak, but she had difficulty in understanding that, because she felt she was much better. Her sufferings had abated somewhat. She remained motionless. Her body was completely wrapped as in a cast. Only her arms were outside the covers, but she could not move them without great pain. Her bloodless hands were cold and white and her feet like ice.

Towards ten o'clock in the evening she seemed to be slipping into a coma. She moaned continually. Dr. Bartoli dropped in again before leaving the hospital for the night. He urged Assunta to go and take some rest. A nurse would remain with Maria. When finally the poor mother agreed to go, the noise of the chair on the stone floor awoke the sufferer. She guessed that her mother was leaving. An effort of protest came to her, but the word was not uttered. **Courageous to the end, she**

THE FINAL STRUGGLE

accepted still another sacrifice.

Throughout the night, in a half-conscious state, she moaned as though hot flames bathed her body. Spasms of pain racked her nerves. Every now and then a convulsion would bring an involuntary cry to her lips. At dawn, exhausted, she fell into a labored sleep.

At five o'clock Dr. Bartoli returned. He found her sleeping. Her respiration was regular but scarcely perceptible. A half-hour later she awoke with a groan. She seemed to remember nothing that had happened. When Assunta entered with the hospital chaplain a light smile passed over Maria's face. She told her mother that she felt well, inquired where she had passed the night, spoke of her brothers and sisters, and said she would like to see them.

Her thoughts went back to Ferriere without any fright. The name of Alexander did not cross her lips, nor did anyone dare recall to her mind the tragic events of the preceding day.

When the priest offered to bring her Holy Communion her face lit up with evident joy. She had been expecting that Visitor. Slowly she crossed her hands on her breast and asked her mother to raise the pillow a bit.

Her soul was ready but there remained one more heroic act before her final tryst with God. The Chaplain reminded her of how Jesus had pardoned His murderers when He died upon the Cross.

She seemed to reflect. Her eyes rested upon

the crucifix on the wall. Then with voice expressive of her generous soul, she explained:

"I, too, pardon him. I, too, wish that he come some day and join me in heaven."

Assunta wept. The Priest too brushed away the tears as he turned to get the Blessed Sacrament. In a few moments he was back and Maria received her dear Jesus in Holy Viaticum.

Ten o'clock that morning Dr. Bartoli returned to change the dressings. Great violet scabs had formed about the wounds. Black and blue lumps now showed on the knees, the legs and elbows, indicating with what desperate fury the child had fought for freedom. But these were only slight injuries compared to the wounds she received. The perforation of the intestines was especially grave. Internal hemorrhages were threatening, blood poisoning that could carry her off within a few hours. The doctor saw by the failing respiration that the end was not far off.

During the morning Sergeant Fantini came to question the victim and draw up a charge against Alexander. Maria answered calmly in monosyllables, without showing the least resentment. When she was asked where the dagger had struck, she pointed very simply to the wounds in her breast, adding modestly, "and elsewhere." He and the Carabiniere dared not inquire further.

When Assunta was again alone with her daughter, she asked if Alexander had not tried to seduce her at other times. Maria admitted simply that there were two other attempts which she had rejected.

"But why didn't you tell me about it?," Assunta pleaded.

"Because he said he would kill me if I did." Then with a sigh, "and you see, he killed me anyway."

By now Maria was failing fast. Extreme Unction was administered, and for three hours she battled with an invisible enemy. Her head swayed on the pillow, her hands clenched.

"Alexander! Alexander, leave me go . . . NO! NO! NO! You will go to hell! Mama, mama, help!" The memory of the struggle haunted her delirium.

Some moments of lucidity pierced through those trying hours. "Mama," she said, "forgive me." The mother's answer was a mother's kiss.

The last agony began at three o'clock in the afternoon. Her eyes settled on the statue of our Lady placed at the foot of her bed. Suddenly her lips stammered, "Theresa". The nurse took her icy hand: "Your baby sister is not here, Maria."

A long spasm shook her whole body, her muscles tensed, she threw back her head violently against the pillow. A long gasp seemed to tear out her lungs. Her head settled calmly on the pillow. The light in her beautiful eyes went out. Maria had breathed her last. God had already rewarded her victory.

It was July 2, 1902, and out over the city, bells were ringing the vesper hour. In the nearby Church Passionists were chanting the antiphon from the Feast of the Precious Blood. Who is this that cometh . . . this beautiful one . . . and why is thy apparel red and thy garments like theirs that tread in the wine press?"

11.

Epilogue

Just forty-eight years later, on June 24, 1950, over two-hundred thousand Holy Year pilgrims thronged the Piazza of the greatest Cathedral of Christianity to hear His Holiness, Pope Pius XII, in the first out-door canonization proclaim Saint Maria Goretti the new patroness of Catholic youth.

Looking up through tear-dimmed eyes at the magnificent picture of Maria in glory was Assunta Goretti. She is the first mother ever to witness her daughter's canonization, and did she perhaps remember in the thrill of that moment what Maria had said to cheer her in the darkest hour at Ferriere . . . "Mama, why are you crying? All will be well . . . we shall be great . . . we shall have everything!"

12.

Model of Youth

(Homily delivered by His Holiness, Pope Pius XII, at the ceremony of Canonization of Saint Maria Goretti, in the Piazza of St. Peter's, June 24, 1950)

By the loving providence of God, we have assisted this evening at the supreme exaltation of a humble daughter of the people, in a ceremony whose solemnity and dignity are unique in the history of the Church. For tonight's canonization has been held in this vast and inviting place of mystery, made for the occasion into a sacred temple whose vault is the open heaven that proclaims the glories of Almighty God—a choice for which you first expressed the desire before We had decided to make the disposition.

The concourse of the faithful come here for the occasion, exceeds anything that has ever been witnessed at any other canonization. You have been lured here, We might almost say, by the entrancing beauty and intoxicating fragrance of this lily mantled with crimson whom We, only a moment ago, had the intense pleasure of inscribing in the roll of the saints: the sweet little martyr of purity, Maria Goretti.

But why, beloved children, have you come here in such countless numbers to assist at her glorification? Why is it that when you read or listen to the story of her brief life, which reminds you of the limpid narrative of the Gospels in the simplicity of its details, in the color of its circumstances, in the sudden violence of death with which it closes—why does this story move you even to tears? Why has Maria Goretti so quickly conquered your hearts, and taken the first place in your affections?

The reason is because there is still in this world, apparently sunk and immersed in the worship of pleasure, not only a meagre little band of chosen souls who thirst for heaven and its pure air —but a crowd, nay, an immense multitude on whom the supernatural fragrance of Christian purity exercises an irresistible and reasuring fascination.

If it is true that in the martyrdom of Maria Goretti there stands out above everything else her purity, it is also true that in her and with her the other Christian virtues are not less glorified. For in her virtue of purity we have the most basic and significant confirmation of the perfect dominion of her spirit over gross matter. In her act of supreme heroism, which was not something unprepared, we see an evidence of her tender and docile love, at once obedient and practical, towards the parents of her flesh. There was also the sacrifice she had made in her difficult daily labor. There was the evangelical poverty to which she freely submitted and in which she was sustained by her confidence in heavenly Providence. There was her religion to which she tenaciously clung and which she desired to understand better with the passing of every day—which she nourished by the practice of her prayers and which thus became for her a veritable treasure in her life. There was her ardent longing to receive Jesus in the Eucharist. Finally, as the crown of her charity, there was the heroic pardon which she granted to the man who had murdered her. A rustic garland of flowers in the field—these virtues—but ever so dear to God, for they adorned the white veil of her First Communion, and shortly after, her martyrdom.

This sacred rite of Canonization has really developed into a spontaneous and popular demonstration in favor of purity. For although against the light of every martyrdom there is, perforce, the ugly contrasting stain of some iniquity, behind that of Maria Goretti stands the spectacle of a scandal that at the beginning of this century was practically unnoticed.

During the past fifty years, coupled with what was often a weak reaction on the part of decent people, there has been a conspiracy of evil practices, propagating themselves in books and illustrations, in theatres and radio programs, in styles and clubs and on the beaches, trying to work their way into the heart of the family and society, and doing their worst damage among the youth, even among those of the tenderest years in whom the possession of virtue is a natural inheritance.

Dearly beloved youth, young men and women, who are the special object of the love of Jesus and of Us, tell me, are you resolved to resist firmly, with the help of Divine grace, against every attempt made to violate your chastity?

You fathers and mothers, tell me—in the presence of this vast multitude, and before the image of this young virgin who by her inviolate candor has stolen your hearts . . . in the presence of her mother who educated her to martyrdom and who, as much as she felt the bitterness of the outrage, never complained about her daughter's death and is now moved with emotion as she invokes her—tell me, are you ready to assume the solemn duty laid upon you to watch, as far as in you lies, over your sons and daughters, to preserve and defend them against so many dangers that surround them, and to keep them always far away from places where they might learn the practices of impiety and of moral perversion?

Finally, all of you who are intently listening to Our Words, know that above the unhealthy marshes and filth of the world, stretches an immense heaven of beauty. It is the heaven which fascinated little Maria; the heaven to which she longed to ascend by the only road that leads there, which is, religion, the love of Christ, and the heroic observance of His commandments.

We greet you, O beautiful and loveable saint! Martyr on earth and angel in heaven, look down from your glory on this people, which loves you, which venerates, glorifies and exalts you. On your forehead you bear the full brilliant and victorious name of Christ. In your virginal countenance may be read the strength of your love and the constancy of your fidelity to your Divine Spouse. As His bride espoused in blood, you have traced in yourself His own image. To you, therefore, powerful intercessor with the Lamb of God, we entrust these Our sons and daughters who are present here, and those countless others who are united with Us in spirit. For while they admire your heroism, they are even more desirous of imitating your strength of faith and your inviolate purity of conduct. Fathers and mothers have recourse to you, asking you to help them in their task of education. In you, through Our hands, the children and all the young people will find a safe refuge, trusting that they shall be protected from every contamination, and be able to walk the highways of life with that serenity of spirit and deep joy which is the heritage of those who are pure of heart. Amen.

13.

Heaven on the Swampland

(Movie version of Maria Goretti's life)

In an attempt to make the movie version of a story more exciting and dramatic, scenario writers too often let their imaginations take over where the facts leave off. But in filming the life-story of Maria Goretti, entitled "Heaven on the Swampland", Augusto Genina found a subject packed with drama and human interest. This Italian producer had no need, therefore, for synthetic excitement, and his resulting picture is quite factually accurate and impressive.

The opening scene shows the Goretti family on their way to Ferriere di Conca, slushing through the swampy plain of the Roman Campagna in a pelting rain. The father, Luigi, is looking for work and has already been turned down by a number of farmers. At length, he is taken in by Count Mazzoleni, owner of a large estate.

The house to which the Count assigns them is a ramshackled affair, and Luigi is dismayed to find that it is in the worst section of the property. Still more disheartening, the Serenellis, Giovanni and Alexander, are pictured as living in the place and bitterly resenting the intrusion of the Gorettis. When old Serenelli tells Luigi to move on, the two men come to blows. Peace is restored by the intervenion of Teresa Cimarelli, a neighbor who shows a friendly interest in the newcomers.

The two families settle down in their new quarters and the next day they go out to work in the fields. Luigi is indefatigable in his efforts to make the land productive, but he is already the victim of the dread malaria. Frequently the disease assails him, but he does not tell the family. Why worry his wife, Assunta, or frighten the children? Surely God will help him carry on.

As the malaria becomes more manifest, Luigi decides to see the doctor in Nettuno and learns that he is a very sick man. Maria, meanwhile, has been invited by Alexander to accompany him to the beach. Since she has never before seen the sea, the girl is quite thrilled. She takes off her shoes and splashes through the water. Alexander conceives a sudden passion for her, but manages to control himself.

Back home clouds of gloom begin to gather. Luigi does not follow the doctor's advice that he rest, but goes out to sow the field. He has a violent attack on the way and they have to lift him out of the cart and lay him on the grass next to the road. The Serenellis hurry away for help, while Maria remains beside him. While they are gone, Luigi gasps his last breath and the picture fades with Maria sobbing over her dead father.

In the next scene Spring has come again. After her father's death, Maria has taken over the housework, while Assunta works in the fields. They have both bravely faced their hard lot, confiding in the help of Heaven. Things become all the more difficult as old Serenelli takes to drink, and Maria discovers that she has become the object of Alexander's interest.

At first the young man seems so nice, offering presents which Maria innocently accepts. But when he suddenly solicits her, the girl refuses absolutely and fights off his clumsy advances. Even the malicious explanations of her girl-friend regarding sin do not shake her determination to remain pure. But all of this seems to arouse Alexander's passion the more, and he threatens to kill Maria if she does not submit to him.

Then some days later, while the others are working in the fields, Alexander surprises Maria in the kitchen and demands that she give in to him or die. The frightened girl knows full well that Alexander is crazed with lust, but still she refuses. In mad frenzy Alexander stabs her, and Maria slumps to the floor with blood seeping through her blouse.

Sobbered by what he has done, Alexander rushes to his room and bolts the door. When Maria is discovered, a cry goes up for her attacker, Alexander. The boy is found and led off to jail, while an ambulance is called to take Maria to the Orsenigo Hospital at Nettuno.

At the hospital the doctors try to save the girl by an operation, but her wounds are too many and too deep. The following afternoon, surrounded by her loved ones, Maria forgives her murderer and dies the death of a saint.

There are slight modifications in the story to suit the exigencies of the film, the picture as a whole is authentic and well worth seeing.

For its beautiful and realistic portrayal of Maria's life, "Heaven on the Swampland" was awarded unanimously the Grand Pize at the 10th International Exhibition of Cinema Art at Venice, 1949. In the opinion of the International jury, it was the film of the year which contributed most to the spiritual and moral betterment of mankind. In all, six Grand Prizes have been awarded this stirring film.

MAP OF ITALY

SENIGALLIA
CORINALDO
ANCONA

ADRIATIC SEA

APENNINE MOUNTAINS

ROME
CAMPO MORTO
FERRIERE DI CONCA
ANZIO
NETTUNO

TYRRHENIAN SEA

MEDITERRANEAN

Daughters of St. Paul

IN MASSACHUSETTS
    50 St. Paul's Avenue, Boston, Ma. 02130
    172 Tremont Street, Boston, Ma. 02111
IN NEW YORK
    78 Fort Place, Staten Island, N.Y. 10301
    59 East 43rd St., New York, N.Y. 10017
    625 East 187th Street, Bronx, N.Y. 10458
    525 Main Street, Buffalo, N.Y. 14203
IN NEW JERSEY
    Hudson Mall — Route 440 and
      Communipaw Ave., Jersey City, N.J. 07304
IN CONNECTICUT
    202 Fairfield Avenue, Bridgeport, Ct. 06604
IN OHIO
    2105 Ontario St. (at Prospect Ave.), Cleveland, Oh. 44115
    25 E. Eighth Street, Cincinnati, Oh. 45202
IN PENNSYLVANIA
    1719 Chestnut St., Philadelphia, Pa. 19103
IN FLORIDA
    2700 Biscayne Blvd., Miami, Fl. 33137
IN LOUISIANA
    4403 Veterans Memorial Blvd., Metairie, La. 70002
    1800 South Acadian Thruway, P.O. Box 2028,
      Baton Rouge, La. 70802
IN MISSOURI
    1001 Pine St. (at North 10th), St. Louis, Mo. 63101
IN TEXAS
    114 East Main Plaza, San Antonio, Tx. 78205
IN CALIFORNIA
    1570 Fifth Avenue, San Diego, Ca. 92101
    46 Geary Street, San Francisco, Ca. 94108
IN HAWAII
    1143 Bishop St., Honolulu, Hi. 96813
IN ALASKA
    750 West 5th Avenue, Anchorage, Ak. 99501
IN CANADA
    3022 Dufferin Street, Toronto 395, Ontario, Canada
IN ENGLAND
    57, Kensington Church Street, London W. 8, England
IN AUSTRALIA
    58, Abbotsford Rd., Homebush, N.S.W., Sydney 2140,
      Australia